John Adams

BRAVE PATRIOT

GROW
with
BOOKS

Scotkovsky

John Adams

BRAVE PATRIOT

by Laurence Santrey
illustrated by Dick Smolinski

Troll Associates

Library of Congress Cataloging in Publication Data

Santrey, Laurence.
    John Adams, brave patriot.

    Summary: A biography of our second President, the
brilliant patriot from Massachusetts.
    1. Adams, John, 1735-1826—Juvenile literature.
2. Presidents—United States—Biography—Juvenile
literature. [1. Adams, John, 1735-1826. 2. Presidents]
I. Smolinski, Dick, ill. II. Title.
E322.S26   1986   973.4 '4 '0924 [B] [92]   85-1095
ISBN 0-8167-0559-3 (lib. bdg.)
ISBN 0-8167-0560-7 (pbk.)

John Adams

BRAVE PATRIOT

In 1776, America declared its independence from Great Britain. John Adams of Massachusetts was one of the new nation's most important leaders.

Yet Adams was not a brave general like George Washington. He was neither a scientist like Benjamin Franklin, nor a gifted writer like Thomas Jefferson, the author of the Declaration of Independence. What, then, made John Adams great?

John Adams, son of John and Susanna Boylston Adams, was born on October 19, 1735, in Braintree, Massachusetts. Braintree was a small village near the Atlantic Ocean, about ten miles south of Boston. The Adams family, like most of their neighbors, were farmers. Mr. Adams was also a cordwainer, or bootmaker.

The sturdy Adams home, which still stands, was built in 1681. Made of wood, it stood two stories high, topped by a sharply peaked roof. The style of the house was called a saltbox. That's because it was shaped like the boxes in which salt was kept in those days. The saltbox was a good design for the snowy Massachusetts winters. As the snow melted, it slid easily from the sharply slanted roof. The Adams house had two large rooms on each floor. Downstairs were the kitchen and the parlor. Upstairs were two bedrooms.

Birthplace of
John Adams

John and Susanna Adams owned many acres of farmland and pastures where their sheep and cows grazed. They had fields of wheat, barley, corn, and vegetables. Most of the land was rich and produced good crops or excellent grass for the animals to eat.

Only one of the Adams's fields was bad. They tried to clear it for farming, but finally gave up. This land they called Stony Acres, a name that fit very well. Even so, John and Susanna Adams decided to keep it. They knew that someday it could be sold for a good price. Land that close to Boston, even if it wasn't good for farming, was valuable.

Stony Acres would go up for sale when Johnny, their first child, was ready for college. The Adams planned to send him to Harvard. It was a family tradition for the eldest Adams son to attend Harvard College, and become a minister. Keeping a student at Harvard until he graduated was expensive. But good old Stony Acres was going to pay for that!

Little Johnny had a happy, secure childhood in Braintree. Before he started school at the age of five, he spent his days roaming around Braintree. He watched the workers planting or harvesting grain. He went down to the shore and watched the fishermen bring in the day's catch. He wandered through the woods, gathering berries or nuts to bring home. As long as the weather was sunny, and there were no chores, Johnny was free to do whatever he wished.

Little Johnny did do his share of chores. The family kept chickens, ducks, and geese, and John was expected to feed them and to keep their living area clean.

Johnny had another regular job. He brought home small, dry twigs and branches for tinder. This wood was kept in a large bucket beside the fireplace. The big logs used for heat and cooking were hard to set ablaze, so tinder was used to start a fire. These burning branches gave off enough heat to start the logs burning.

Sometimes Johnny had an extra job. When the fire went out during the night, he was sent to a neighbor with a covered pan. He told the neighbor what happened and asked for some burning wood, which he brought home in the pan. It was common for hearth fires to go out, and just as common for neighbors to send over a new flame, or starter, this way. It was normal to see children hurrying between houses early in the morning, carefully carrying a pan or shovel.

When Johnny was five, he began attending school. His first schoolhouse was on Penn Hill, right across the road from the Adams house. It was an elementary school, run by a woman called Dame Belcher. Mrs. Belcher was a widow who taught reading, writing, and arithmetic to the youngest boys and girls of Braintree.

For most children of that time, education ended when they left elementary school, at the age of nine or ten. Not many went on to secondary school. Elementary schools in New England were public and did not charge tuition, or money. The taxes a family paid to its town covered the costs of elementary school. Secondary schools, however, did charge tuition, and that made it impossible for most children to attend.

Johnny was a bright child. He taught himself to read before he started school. He enjoyed Mrs. Belcher's classes and everything she

taught. Dame Belcher was a kind woman with a sense of humor, and Johnny liked her. He often stayed after school, just to talk with and help his teacher.

Dame Belcher had a corn field next to her house. Every week during the fall months, she took corn to the mill. There, the miller ground up the corn so it could be used to make bread or porridge. Johnny gladly carried each sack of corn to the mill and brought it back, all ground. For this, Dame Belcher paid him three pennies. Each time she handed him the coins, she said, "Save your pennies, Johnny, and buy land with it."

Johnny knew that land was valuable and a good thing to have. His mother and father told him that. But there was another way the little boy wanted to spend his money. The local store had shiny penny-whistles, colorful kites, balls, ice skates, and other nice things. Sometimes Johnny could buy what he wanted right away. Sometimes he had to save for several weeks.

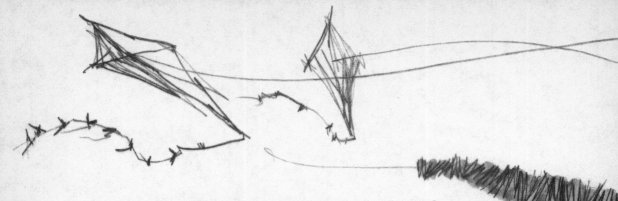

Johnny and his friends enjoyed many different games. They played hopscotch, flew kites, danced around the Maypole, raced on the ice-covered pond. They also played marbles, blind man's buff, tag, and badminton. Colonial children also had a game called base-ball, but we don't know if it was anything like modern baseball. We do know, however, that Johnny and his friends enjoyed different sports and games in different seasons.

For example, the time for playing marbles came in January. It was followed by the top-spinning season, which was followed by kite time. Kite flying ended around April Fool's Day. Ball playing in New England began on the first Thursday in April. Nobody knows who started the seasons for different sports, or why. But Johnny and his friends didn't worry about that. They just enjoyed playing.

When he was an adult, John Adams remembered his early years as joyful. He loved his parents and his younger brothers, Peter and Elihu. He had many friends and plenty to do. He went fishing and horseback riding, played sports, and swam. School was wonderful, too, because Dame Belcher was so nice and the work never seemed hard.

The fun stopped when Johnny was about ten years old. His parents enrolled him in the Latin School, a secondary school run by Mr. Joseph Cleverly. Mr. Cleverly was the opposite of Dame Belcher. She was kind, loved children, and made learning a pleasure. Mr. Cleverly did not like children, had no interest in his work, and made learning dull and lifeless. Mr. Cleverly, who had just graduated from Harvard, was not a cruel man. He simply felt that he was too intelligent and scholarly to be teaching young people.

Classes at the Latin School consisted almost completely of learning the book *Latin Grammar* from eight o'clock in the morning to five o'clock in the afternoon. Studying grammar meant memorizing Latin verbs, nouns, and so on. Not until the entire book was learned by heart was a student allowed to go on to anything else. The Latin School was also supposed to teach Greek, geography, English, and mathematics. But Mr. Cleverly rarely bothered with any of those subjects. He just instructed his students to read and memorize their Latin grammar.

When Johnny went to Dame Belcher's school, he couldn't wait to tell his parents everything he had learned. Now that he was at the Latin School, his conversation never included any mention of school or what he was learning. After a while his parents noticed, but they said nothing. If John had a complaint, they felt, he would tell them when he was ready.

John did not complain about school, even though he disliked it. He knew that the entrance examination for Harvard required knowledge of Latin, which meant he had to learn it. After two years, however, John couldn't stand it anymore. He told his father that he didn't like to study, and wanted to go to work on the farm. Mr. Adams was disappointed, but didn't try to change John's mind. Instead, he suggested that John dig a ditch for him in one of their meadows.

"This seemed a delightful change," John Adams wrote years later, "and to the meadow I went—But I soon found ditching harder than Latin, and the first forenoon[1] was the longest I ever experienced. That day I ate the bread of labor, and glad was I when night came on. That night I made comparison between Latin grammar and ditching, but said not a word about it. I dug the next forenoon, and wanted to return to Latin at dinner, but it was humiliating, and I could not do it. At night toil conquered

pride, and I told my father, one of the severest trials of my life, that, if he chose, I would go back to Latin grammar.''

Mr. Adams was pleased that John had learned a lesson by experience. Learning by experience was much better than lectures, punishment, or

force. And John had certainly learned the lesson. Even as an adult, he never forgot those two days in the meadow. Whatever hard tasks he faced— as a lawyer, a member of the Continental Congress, a diplomat, Vice President, and then President of the United States—nothing was ever as difficult to him as digging a ditch in that stony New England soil.

Twelve-year-old John Adams returned to his studies with a new attitude. He was going to learn his Latin and be well-prepared for the Harvard examination. John and one of his Latin School classmates, John Hancock, sometimes groaned to each other about Mr. Cleverly's dull classes. They felt they should be studying other things besides grammar. So many developments were taking place in England and the Colonies, yet they weren't learning anything about these events. To Mr. Cleverly, history and government meant only the history and government of ancient Rome. The boys also wanted to know about the present.

The adults John Adams knew were involved in politics and the community. Braintree, like every other Massachusetts village and town, held regular public meetings. At these gatherings, all the citizens discussed and voted on important issues. Even when there wasn't an official public meeting, politics was the focus of many local conversations.

The Adams house was often filled with neighbors and relatives sitting in front of the fireplace on cold winter evenings. They argued about England's King George III and Parliament, and the Massachusetts colony. John sat quietly and listened. He heard some of the adults praise the king. After all, the king had never interfered with the way the colonists lived and governed themselves. At the same time, these Loyalists said, the king protected them from the French, the Spanish, the Indians, and other threats to their well-being.

Others in the group disagreed. They argued that things could change. The Colonies held

vast, untapped riches. Who could tell if the king would let the colonists keep all this wealth to themselves? The colonists were starting to build ships and develop their own industries. Would the British allow this independent behavior? These questions stayed in John's head long after the adults left, and he lay in bed thinking about them for many hours.

Young John worked hard at his studies, but felt he could be learning more. He was eager to start mathematics, and was disappointed that Mr. Cleverly was not teaching it. To do something about that, the youngster borrowed a math book from school and went to work on his own. He studied algebra, trigonometry, decimals, and interest rates. He asked his parents to pose real problems, so he could solve them by using math.

Every night, after supper, John sat on a stool in front of the kitchen fireplace. He balanced a small writing desk on his lap and worked at the problems. All this effort was rewarded. As John Adams wrote later, "I went through the whole course, overtook and passed by all the scholars at school, without any master."

Unfortunately, John knew he would not be able to teach himself enough of the Latin and Greek he needed to know to get into Harvard. The college's entrance examination would be hard. The exam was given by the president and two instructors, who took turns quizzing the applicant, or student.

One examiner selected a book by Virgil, Tully, or some other ancient writer, and chose a passage. The young applicant would have to read the passage aloud, translate it into English, and explain what it meant. Another examiner chose a passage in English, to be translated into Latin. The third examiner asked the applicant to show understanding and knowledge of Greek. The college hopeful might also be asked to write a poem in Latin, or translate a passage from the New Testament, which was written in Greek. The examiners could ask just about anything, and the applicant had to be ready to answer them.

John was so worried that he would fail the
test that he asked his father if he could leave
Mr. Cleverly's school and go to Joseph Marsh's
school. Mr. Marsh ran a private school near the
Adams farm. John's father did not like Mr.
Marsh. Mr. Adams felt that Marsh was too
critical of the king and the British government.

Most of the citizens of Braintree, including
Mr. Adams, believed that all problems between
the Colonies and England could be settled

reasonably. Mr. Marsh disagreed. He said that revolution was coming, that Braintree's citizens were fooling themselves if they thought the king would give in without a struggle.

Mr. Adams was sure that Mr. Marsh's ideas were wrong, but there was no doubt that Marsh was a fine teacher. His students had no trouble with the Harvard entrance examination. So, Mr. Adams enrolled his fourteen-year-old son in Mr. Marsh's school.

On John's first day of classes, Mr. Marsh had the teen-ager read from a Latin textbook. It was clear that John knew almost no Latin except grammar. Even so, it was also clear that he was a bright youngster who could learn quickly. Mr. Marsh assured John, right then, that he would pass the college examination in one year—if he was willing to work hard.

John got started immediately, and advanced rapidly in his studies. Learning was again the pleasure it had been at Dame Belcher's school. Mr. Marsh and John got along very well. They were alike in many ways. Both used words with wit and precision. Both were great readers and liked to argue about books, ideas, and people. John's feelings about the colonists' loyalty to the king began to change under Mr. Marsh's influence. The boy had thought about loyalty and liberty before, but had never dared to put his ideas into words. Now, with Joseph Marsh encouraging him, the teen-ager let his mind run free. In later years, John Adams recognized how much he owed to the clear-thinking, independent schoolmaster.

On July 5, 1751, when John was almost sixteen, he took the entrance examination for Harvard College. John was worried as he waited to face his examiners, but the eighteen other applicants were equally nervous. John was glad of one thing. He would not have to wait to find out whether he passed or failed. An applicant who passed was given a composition to write at home, and the school rules to be copied and memorized. Later that day, John was overjoyed to be given a composition assignment. He couldn't wait to get home to tell his parents and Joseph Marsh that he would attend college in the fall. With great pleasure, Mr. and Mrs. Adams sold Stony Acres to help pay for John's college education.

41

John Adams spent the next four years as a Harvard student. In that time, he realized that he did not want to enter the ministry. He wasn't certain what he wanted to be, just that he was eager to learn. The classes were interesting, the library was filled with marvelous books, and John met many young students from different parts of the Colonies. Until this time, he had not known anyone who wasn't a citizen of Massachusetts. Now, he heard the thoughts of people from New York, Georgia, Virginia, and the other colonies. He discussed politics with them at every opportunity.

In those four years, John Adams changed the way he thought. Before college, he considered himself a citizen of Massachusetts. Now, he was beginning to see himself as an American, united with other Americans from the other twelve colonies. John knew that each colony had its own geography, industries, and ways of life. But he also saw that all the colonies shared the same major problem—the oppression of the English

government. There were thirteen separate colonies, each dealing with England on its own. Being separate made them weak.

John Adams began to think of what might happen if those thirteen colonies joined together to deal with King George. Adams wasn't yet thinking in terms of a revolution and the formation of a free and separate nation. But the seed had been planted in his mind.

After he was graduated close to the top of his class, John Adams became a schoolmaster in Worcester, Massachusetts. The next year, 1756, he began to study law. In those days, there were no law schools. Instead, a would-be lawyer worked as a clerk for an attorney, and read law books. To become a practicing lawyer, the student then had to prove knowledge of the law to a panel of examiners. John Adams did so and was accepted as a lawyer in Boston on November 6, 1758.

In the years that followed, John became well-known as a brilliant trial lawyer. He also gained a reputation as a clever and persuasive speaker and writer on politics. He felt so strongly about American independence that he called himself "John Yankee."

In 1771, Adams held his first public office, as a member of the Massachusetts House of Representatives. Three years later, he joined the Continental Congress, which was meeting in Philadelphia. There, he proposed that George Washington be designated Commander-in-Chief of the Continental Army. In the months that followed, John Adams played a major role in the drafting of the Declaration of Independence, and the formation of the new United States government. During this time, Adams and Thomas Jefferson became close friends. It was a friendship that would last for many years to come.

John Adams was Minister to France during the American Revolution, and Minister to Great Britain after the war. In 1788, when George Washington was elected the first President of the United States, Adams was his Vice President. They both served for two terms. Adams then served one term as President of the United States, the first President to live in the White House.

In March 1801, when Adams left the Presidency, he went back to his childhood home in Braintree. There, he spent the next twenty-five years as a respected elder statesman. One of the highlights of Adams' later years was the correspondence he maintained with Thomas Jefferson. Their friendship continued until July 4, 1826. It was on that day, the fiftieth anniversary of the signing of the Declaration of Independence, that John Adams died. His last words were "Thomas Jefferson still survives."

He could not know that Jefferson had died that morning. Two of the nation's greatest patriots had died on the same day, and they were mourned by all Americans.

47

John Adams gave much to his country. As President, John Adams kept America out of war. He believed keeping America at peace was his greatest accomplishment.

During the Revolution, he knew he would lose his property, perhaps his life, if the British won. But he never hesitated to raise his voice among the leaders crying for liberty.